The Causes of World War I

Tony Allan

Heinemann Library
Chicago, Illinois

Produced for Heinemann Library by Discovery Books
Designed by Ian Winton
Illustrated by Stefan Chabluk
Consultant: Stewart Ross
Picture research by Rachel Tisdale
Originated by Dot Gradations
Printed by Wing King Tong in Hong Kong

07 06 05 04 03
10 9 8 7 6 5 4 3 2 1

Library of Congress Cataloging-in-Publication Data
Allan, Tony, 1967-
   The causes of World War I / Tony Allan.
      p. cm. -- (20th-century perspectives)
Summary: Explores key topics involving World War I and shows the causes
that led up to the outbreak of war, including France's defeat in the
Franco-Prussian War, the assassination of Franz Ferdinand, the heir to
the Austro-Hungarian throne, and Germany's attack on France.
Includes bibliographical references and index.
   ISBN 1-40340-148-9
   1. World War, 1914-1918--Causes--Juvenile literature. [1. World War,
1914-1918--Causes.] I. Title: Causes of World War One. II. Title:
Causes of World War 1. III. Title. IV. Series.
   D511 .A698 2002
   940.3'11--dc21
                                        2002004362

Acknowledgments
The publishers would like to thank the following for permission to reproduce photographs:
pp. 4, 6, 17, 21, 32, 35, 43 Hulton Getty; pp. 5, 13, 18, 22, 28, 31, 40 Peter Newark; pp. 8, 9, 10,
12, 14, 16, 20, 24, 25, 26, 29, 30, 33, 38 Mary Evans; p. 11 David King Collection; p. 15 Hulton
Deutsch; p. 19 Corbis; p. 27 Popperfoto; pp. 34, 37, 42 Hulton Archive; p. 39 Art Archive.

Cover photograph reproduced with permission of Hulton Archive. On the cover of this book,
Austria's Archduke Franz Ferdinand and his wife, Sophie, are shown in Sarajevo on June 28, 1914, the
day they were both shot by an assassin.

Every effort has been made to contact copyright holders of any material reproduced in this book.
Any omissions will be rectified in subsequent printings if notice is given to the publishers.

Some words are shown in bold, **like this.** You can find out what they
mean by looking in the glossary.

Contents

What Was World War I?

Saturday, July 1, 1916, dawned sunny above the trenches in northern France. For many months, British and French forces had been confronting German troops, who were similarly dug in, across a ravaged wasteland a few hundred yards wide. Then, at 7:30 A.M., the order came for the British troops to rush out of the trenches and go "over the top." Their commanders had decided that the only way out of the bloody **stalemate** was an all-out assault. So the Battle of the Somme began.

Over the next four months, the war-torn meadows north of the Somme River in northern France were home to killing on a massive scale. Soldiers on both sides were **raked** by rifle and machine-gun fire as they surged across **no-man's-land.** When the battle finally drew to a close at the end of October, British **casualties** amounted to 420,000, French to almost 200,000, and German to around 500,000—a total of more than one million men. In return for the sacrifice, the British and French forces had managed to win back about six miles (ten kilometers) of barren, shattered wasteland.

Scottish troops go "over the top," leaving the trenches to launch an attack on the German front line during the Battle of the Somme.

Trench warfare

Much of the fighting in World War I took place in and between trenches—deep ditches protected by barbed wire. When soldiers were in the trenches, it was called being "dug in." It was from these trenches that armies launched attacks on each other. Once soldiers left the relative safety of the trenches by going "over the top," there was little to protect them from enemy fire. Soldiers defending their own trenches were often armed with machine guns that could fire hundreds of bullets every minute. This led to many more of the attacking soldiers being killed than the soldiers defending the trenches.

The war that changed the world

The Battle of the Somme was only one of dozens of violent confrontations in World War I. The war involved not just French, German, and British forces but also, among others, Austrians, Hungarians, Russians, Italians, Turks, Australians, New Zealanders, and Canadians. For the last nineteen months of the war, the Americans also joined. Until then, the United States had followed what historians call a policy of isolation, because they wanted to keep out of any European conflict. The human cost of World War I, which finally came to an end in November 1918, was mind-boggling. About 10 million soldiers were killed, with the greatest losses suffered by the Germans, who had 1.8 million killed, and the Russians, who lost 1.7 million soldiers.

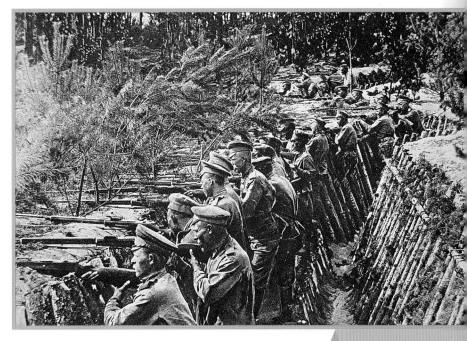

Russian forces wait for an attack on their trench on the Eastern Front in 1917. The wooden supports stopped the sides of the trenches from collapsing.

Causes of catastrophe

The scale of the tragedy was so great that, even before the war was over, people on both sides were arguing fiercely over what could have caused the catastrophe. At the time, they tended to blame their enemies. Eventually, people on both sides came to realize that the roots of the conflict lay deep in the long-term rivalries of competing European countries. They saw the system of **alliances** that bound different countries together and the general buildup of armies and weapons as other possible causes of the war. World War I may have broken out abruptly, but the causes of conflict had begun several decades earlier.

An English soldier writes home

English soldier Lieutenant Will Mulholland wrote a letter home describing what he saw on the Somme battlefront: *"Shall I tell you of the horrors—deaths in every form some calm and placid, some blasted and vaporized, some mutilated, one almost burnt to a cinder by me in a dugout?"*

Background to the Tragedy

At the start of the twentieth century, Europe was easily the richest and most powerful region of the world. This was the time of **colonial** empires, when European countries ruled much of the globe. Europe owed its greatness to the new wealth and progress created by the **Industrial Revolution.** Starting in Great Britain in the late eighteenth century, the revolution had spread across the continent throughout the nineteenth century, bringing new industries, fresh inventions, and increased job opportunities. But while some countries, such as Britain and Germany, had been in the forefront of economic progress, others, such as Russia, had lagged behind.

Rulers of the world

Above all, Europeans were self-confident. Europe's growing numbers of educated citizens believed they were living in the "Age of Progress," a time they thought all problems could be solved by reason and clear thinking. As pioneers of educated thought and economic development, Europeans believed that they had a duty to spread their civilization around the globe and used this belief to justify colonial rule. Although it was already clear that some non-European powers, most notably the United States and possibly also Japan, were catching up fast, many Europeans in 1900 truly believed that they ruled the world.

Czar Nicholas II of Russia (left) shares a carriage with Kaiser Wilhelm II of Germany while on a state visit to Berlin in 1913. The two men were cousins by marriage. The kaiser was also closely related to King George V of Britain—they were both grandsons of Britain's Queen Victoria.

Few people at the time imagined that a terrible war was on the horizon that would throw European civilization into turmoil. Fewer still could have foreseen that such a disaster would be triggered by a single act of violence. The event that triggered the war occurred on June 28, 1914, in Sarajevo, the capital of Bosnia and Herzegovina. Bosnia and Herzegovina at the time was a province of the Austro-Hungarian Empire.

Descent into disaster

On that day, Archduke Franz Ferdinand, the heir to the Austro-Hungarian throne, was **assassinated** by a terrorist during a ceremonial visit to Sarajevo. Blaming neighboring Serbia for the attack, Austria-Hungary declared war on Serbia. Russia, Serbia's **ally,** then came to Serbia's defense. When Russia started calling up its troops, Austria-Hungary's long-term ally and northern neighbor Germany believed itself also to be at risk. Fearing that it might be trapped in a war on two fronts, against both Russia and Russia's western ally, France, Germany's military leaders insisted on a lightning assault on France. This could only be achieved by striking through **neutral** Belgium. So, on August 4, 1914, German troops swept into Belgium. In defense of Belgium, Great Britain then declared war on Germany. Just 37 days after the archduke's murder in Sarajevo, almost all of Europe was at war. France, Russia, and Britain, called the "Allies," were lined up against Germany and Austria-Hungary, called the **"Central Powers."**

Events moved very quickly, and historians argue even today about why the powers acted as they did. To make sense of what happened in those weeks, it is necessary to try to understand the ambitions, hopes, and fears of each of the countries involved.

Austria-Hungary: Patchwork Empire

The country that set the slide into war in motion was actually the weakest of the great powers. Of the five leading countries that found themselves at war, Austria-Hungary had the smallest military budget and one of the smaller armies. Although it included areas of heavy industry, particularly around its twin capitals of Vienna and Budapest, much of the country's territory was still used for farming.

Austria-Hungary also faced difficult political problems. Its neighbor Germany was a newly established **nation-state** whose people shared the same language and history. By contrast, the Austro-Hungarian Empire was made up of people who spoke many languages and had different customs and histories. The empire had been expanded by its ruling family, the Habsburgs, who had held power in its Austrian heartland since 1282. Over the centuries they had built up their domains through war, marriage, and **diplomacy,** uniting many groups of people into one nation. However, because of their differences, there was little to link all these people, other than their sometimes uncertain loyalty to the emperor. Since 1848, that emperor had been Franz Joseph. He was 84 years old when war broke out in 1914. Franz Ferdinand, the murdered archduke, had been his nephew and heir.

Emperor Franz Joseph was 84 years old when war broke out in 1914. He had been ruling Austria since 1848.

The rising tide of nationalism

Because of the many different cultures within its borders, Austria-Hungary was particularly at risk from the rising tide of **nationalism** that had swept across Europe in the course of the 19th century. In 1848, known in Europe as the "Year of Revolutions," many of the people who made up the empire, including Hungarians, Czechs, Croatians, Romanians, and Austrians, had risen up in revolt against the Habsburgs. The various uprisings had been stopped violently. In Hungary, for example, the revolt was suppressed only when Russia's **Czar** Nicholas I sent a force of 200,000 soldiers to help his fellow emperor. Then, from 1859 on, the people of the Habsburgs' Italian lands had successfully broken away to join the independent kingdom of Italy.

From the 1870s on, Emperor Franz Joseph's main concern had been with **Slav** people in the southern parts of the Austro-Hungarian empire. For centuries, the Slav lands had come under the control of the **Ottoman** Empire, ruled by **sultans** from Constantinople, (now called Istanbul, Turkey). The sultans' power had weakened during the 19th century, so Austria-Hungary was able to take control of some formerly Ottoman lands. By 1900, Slavs made up nearly half of the total population of Austria-Hungary, but many Slavs were unhappy with this situation and wanted to rule themselves.

Austria-Hungary's concerns over its Slav peoples grew toward the end of the nineteenth century. Serbia, a strong, independent Slav country on Austria-Hungary's southern borders, gained independence from Ottoman Turkey after the **Balkan** crisis of 1878. At first, Serbia's rulers looked to Austria-Hungary for support. But in 1903 a new, more nationalistic ruler took over power in Serbia. From then on, the Austro-Hungarian authorities were convinced that the Serbs were working to undermine the loyalty of the Austro-Hungarian Slavic people to Austria-Hungary and Franz Joseph.

A magazine illustration of 1908 shows women in Serbian clothing learning to handle rifles. Serb nationalism was a powerful force in the years before World War I.

The "sick man of Europe"

During the seventeenth century, the Ottoman Empire, centered on Turkey, had covered large parts of eastern Europe and the Middle East. In the nineteenth century its power began to crumble and it became known as the "sick man of Europe." Some regions of the Ottoman Empire gained independence, such as Greece, Serbia, and Romania. Other parts of the empire were simply taken over by neighboring states.

Russia: Slumbering Giant

Like Austria-Hungary, Russia was an empire of many different races and cultures. Three centuries of expansion had stretched its borders from Germany in the west to the Pacific Ocean in the east. Physically, it was vast, covering one-seventh of the world's land area. More than half its land area was actually in Asia rather than Europe. As a result, fewer than half of Russia's people spoke Russian as their first language.

Everyone knew that in the event of war, Russia would be a hard country to defeat. One conqueror who tried and failed to do so in the 19th century was the French leader Napoleon Bonaparte. After conquering all of continental Europe, he set his sights on Russia. He invaded and captured Moscow in 1811–1812, but the sheer size of the nation and its freezing winter weather had forced him to retreat. He lost most of his men along the way.

In 1905, Japanese forces celebrated a victory over Russia in East Asia in the Russo-Japanese War, which had begun in 1904.

The Russian steamroller

Russia's population was huge. By 1900, it had 130 million people, more than twice as many as Germany and three times the population of Great Britain or France. The peacetime strength of its army amounted to almost one and a half million men, while in war it could count on calling up another five million reservists, or men who would be ready to become soldiers. The Russian army was nicknamed the "steamroller" because it was seen to be slow to start but unstoppable once it got going. The belief that the Russian steamroller would eventually flatten all opposition was widespread across Europe, causing particular alarm in Austria-Hungary and Germany, the countries to the west of Russia.

Infinite resources

In respect for Russia's vast size, Britain's foreign minister, Sir Edward Grey, felt able to insist in a letter to France's president, Raymond Poincaré, shortly before World War I broke out that, *"Russian resources are so great that in the long run Germany will be exhausted without our helping Russia."*

Yet for all its huge size, Russia's army had not been particularly successful in military terms. In the 1850s, it had been defeated on its own territory by French and British forces in the **Crimean War.** A worse shock came in 1904–1905, when Russia was defeated by the relatively small country of Japan in the Russo-Japanese War.

Shattered barricades litter a street in the Russian capital of St. Petersburg during an uprising in 1905. The rioting broke out after Russia's shocking defeat by Japan.

Lagging behind

In fact, there were many weaknesses in the Russian system. The **czar** held absolute power over a land largely made up of **illiterate** peasants. While other nations had brought in required schooling and **democratic** reform, Russia had lagged behind. **Industrialization** had also started late in Russia. In 1900, the nation produced only one-tenth as much coal as Germany and one-fifth as much steel.

These weaknesses affected the nation's military strength. The army was poorly equipped because factories could not produce enough weapons to keep it adequately supplied. Troop transportation was another problem. Russia had only a tenth of the railroad lines per square mile as its western rivals. To add to these considerable problems, the army was often poorly led by officers who had been promoted for their social standing rather than their ability. Russia's minister for war from 1909 to 1915, Vladimir Sukhomlinov, liked to boast, "Look at me! I haven't read a military manual for the last 25 years." But for all its weaknesses, Russia remained a force feared by the rest of Europe.

Not enough weapons

When war broke out in 1914, Russia had only 60 artillery batteries, which are groups of guns used together, compared with 381 in the German army. Each of Russia's guns was supplied with only 850 shells while most other European armies supplied their guns with more than 2,000.

Germany: Insecure Superpower

As a great power, Germany was a relative newcomer in 1914. The country had been officially formed in 1871, when Wilhelm I had been crowned emperor of a newly united land. Previously, the lands of German-speaking people had been a collection of **principalities** and minor kingdoms.

Germany's Iron Chancellor

The man who did the most to unite Germany was the **aristocratic** politician Otto von Bismarck, who became known as the "Iron Chancellor." In 1862, he became prime minister of Prussia, the most powerful of the German states. Determined to create a united German realm under Prussian rule, he fought three short, successful wars over the next nine years. The first was against Denmark, the second against Austria, and the third—the Franco-Prussian War of 1870–71—against France. It was after the Prussian victory over France that the new German Empire was proclaimed on January 18, 1871.

A painting of a German iron factory dated 1900. Such industries helped to increase the wealth of the nation and made it possible for Germany to produce more weapons.

Having achieved his ambitions by war, Bismarck devoted his remaining nineteen years as leader of a united Germany to holding on to his gains by keeping the peace. He did so by maintaining a complicated series of **alliances.** The main goal of these alliances above all was to isolate France, which was still bitter over its costly 1871 defeat. In return for peace, France had been forced to hand over to Germany the two provinces of Alsace and Lorraine, along with a huge cash payment.

In contrast to his relationship with France, Bismarck mended relations with the Austrians. He created the League of the Three Emperors in 1872, which was a friendly agreement between the emperors of Germany, Russia, and Austria-Hungary. In 1879 Bismarck forged the more important Dual Alliance with Austria-Hungary. Three years later, he persuaded Italy to join, making it a **Triple Alliance.**

Bismarck's long hold on power in Germany finally came to an end in 1890, two years after a new emperor (called the "kaiser" in Germany) came to the throne. Born with a withered left arm, Kaiser Wilhelm II combined moods of boundless ambition and self-confidence with periods of doubt. In Wilhelm's hands, German **diplomacy** suddenly changed direction.

The most dynamic country in Europe

The Germany that Wilhelm II inherited was the most dynamic country in Europe. Its industries were thriving, and its educational system was the best in the world. A tightly disciplined army, 2.2 million strong when fully **mobilized,** defended the country. Germany's military successes had encouraged fresh ambition, but the unification of the country had come too late for it to build up a huge **colonial** empire like Great Britain's, and many Germans resented this.

Bismarck's victories had also increased the army's already high prestige. Prussia, in particular, remained the kind of society where pedestrians would step out of the way in respect if an army officer walked by. Wilhelm's own love of everything military and his desire to extend Germany's empire led many in Europe to believe that he had ideas of world domination.

Kaiser Wilhelm II strikes a military pose in this portrait by P. A. Laszlo. His left arm, shown holding a sword, had in fact been withered from birth.

Blood and iron

Shortly after taking power as prime minister of Prussia, Bismarck gave a speech in which he said: *"Not by speeches and majorities will the great questions of the day be decided . . . but by blood and iron."* This view was to have a lingering influence on German policy up to 1914.

France: Wounded Glory

France's fate in the nineteenth century was almost the reverse of Germany's. Where Germany found fresh prestige and strength, France suffered a decline in power and influence. The nation was used to glory. Under Louis XIV, known as the Sun King, France had dominated late seventeenth-century Europe, while in the eighteenth century the language of civilized people across the continent had been French. The French Revolution, which swept away the monarchy in 1789, was unable to provide a stable government. By the end of the century, Napoleon Bonaparte had come to power and soon set about conquering Europe.

Political divisions

After Napoleon's final defeat in 1815, political instability again became a problem. In the course of the 19th century, France saw seven changes of regime, from republic to empire to monarchy and back to republic. In 1871, after France's defeat in the Franco-Prussian War, the **Third Republic** was established. But even after that, there were constant changes of government. The nation had thirteen different foreign ministers from 1871 to 1890. Nevertheless, France bounced back from the disaster of the **Franco-Prussian War** surprisingly quickly. It managed to pay off the **war debt** to Germany in just three years. But the bitterness of the defeat remained, permanently souring relations between the two countries.

Following France's defeat in the Franco-Prussian War, Wilhelm I of Prussia is proclaimed emperor of a united Germany in the Hall of Mirrors at the Palace of Versailles. This palace, situated outside Paris, was once the home of French kings.

A gaping wound

The loss of Alsace and part of Lorraine to Germany after the Franco-Prussian War left France with an enduring sense of loss. Leon Gambetta, the statesman who did most to restore French fortunes after the defeat, once said, *"Never speak of it; think of it always."* France finally regained the lost provinces at the end of World War I.

A capital of culture

French citizens had much to be proud of during the Third Republic. Their culture still led Europe, thanks to the work of great writers such as Victor Hugo, Gustave Flaubert, Emile Zola, and Marcel Proust, musicians like Debussy and Ravel, and artists like Monet, Renoir, Cezanne, and Gauguin. In addition France, and in particular its capital Paris, was known around the world for its fashionable ways of life. In the United States, people would joke, "When good Americans die, they go to Paris."

In this 1899 photo, British and Egyptian flags fly at Fashoda in the Sudan. A confrontation between French and British colonial forces took place there in 1898.

Economically, the country made some progress, though it was still outpaced by its rival Germany. By 1914, France was producing only a third as much iron and steel as its bigger neighbor. Of even more concern was the decline in its population. In 1870 the two countries had roughly the same number of people, but by 1914 France had around 38 million people compared with Germany's 65 million and Austria-Hungary's 52 million.

A colonial power

Politically, France was still a world player. The country had a sizeable **colonial** empire, which by 1900 stretched over four million square miles (ten million square kilometers), in Africa, Indochina, the Caribbean, and other parts of the world. It was second in size only to the British Empire. France's colonial ambitions at times brought the country into conflict with Great Britain. In 1898 the two nations almost went to war over possession of the Sudan. By 1904, however, Britain and France had settled their colonial differences. They both began to feel more threatened by Germany than they did by each other.

Great Britain: Colonial Flag Bearer

This map, issued to celebrate King Edward VII's coronation in 1902, shows the territories of the British Empire (colored pink) stretching around the world. People boasted that the sun never set on the imperial lands.

As an island nation, Great Britain's outlook on the world was always different from that of its neighbors and rivals on the European continent. Over a period of centuries, some of its most ambitious citizens had sought opportunities for trade and expansion overseas. The result was the British Empire, a gradual accumulation of **colonies** and **protectorates** that by the late 19th century stretched all around the globe. The empire included Canada, southern Africa, Australia, and India.

In many ways, the empire was a source of strength for Britain. It provided **raw materials** for British industry and a market in which finished goods produced by British firms could be sold. Partly as a result of its pioneering role in the **Industrial Revolution,** Britain at the turn of the century was one of the wealthiest countries in the world. The nation produced as much iron as Germany and Austria-Hungary combined, and as much coal as all the major European powers put together. However, both Germany and the United States were catching up fast, and in steel production as well as in newer technologies such as chemicals and electricity generation, Germany was already ahead.

Protecting the empire

The need to protect the colonies had shaped British **foreign policy** for much of the nineteenth century. The nation had fought a string of colonial wars in Africa, India, and East Asia. Britain also suspected Russia of having ambitions in central Asia and felt this might threaten Britain's colonial territory in India.

Master of the seas

Of all the armed services, the navy was particularly important to Britain, for without it the empire could not survive. In the days before air travel, only the navy could guarantee the passage of troops, administrators, and trade goods to and from Britain. To ensure that "Britannia ruled the waves," as it used to

George V, the king of Great Britain from 1910 to 1936, visits Bombay, India, in 1911. He was also known as the emperor of India.

be said, the nation's military planners insisted in the 1890s that the British navy should be maintained to the "two-power standard"—in other words, as large as any two other navies put together.

Concerned with protecting the empire, Britain's rulers were wary of becoming involved in European affairs. One government official even boasted of Britain's "splendid isolation," meaning that the country was unaffected by the **alliances** that bound the other European powers in what was becoming a very complicated web.

Yet Britain did have concerns about the political situation in Europe, and these had influenced its foreign policy for hundreds of years. Britain wanted European countries to maintain a **balance of power** so that no single nation would become strong enough to dominate all the others.

Jingoism

The term "jingoism" comes from a song that was popular at the time of the **Balkan** conflict of 1878. It describes an attitude of wild **patriotism.** The following lines are from the song:

> "We don't want to fight, but, by Jingo, if we do,
> we've got the ships, we've got the men, and got the money too."

United States: Reluctant Colossus

As the European powers competed for prestige and influence, one nation that kept itself apart was the United States. Separated from Europe by the 2,813 mile (4,500-kilometer) divide of the Atlantic Ocean, Americans for the most part considered themselves well rid of European squabbling. Most U.S. citizens were recent immigrants or descendants of immigrants who had left the Old World to seek a new life in the United States, and they were mostly glad to leave Europe's problems behind them. American politicians liked to contrast the openness of America's **democratic, republican** society with Europe's social system, where power was still based on **aristocratic** privilege.

A nation on the rise

Yet, whatever its wishes, the United States could not remain entirely unaffected by events in Europe and the rest of the world. The nation had undergone a remarkable change in the last four decades of the nineteenth century. The population of the United States had soared from 32 million in 1860 to 76 million in 1900, and it was continuing to rise by more than one million every year. In comparison, Germany had 56 million people and Great Britain had 41 million. The United States was also vastly wealthier, for **industrialization** had made it a world leader in economic terms. The nation produced more coal than Germany and almost as much steel as Germany and Great Britain combined.

As the American economy grew, foreign trade increased. In turn, the growth of trade bound the United States to what was happening elsewhere in the world. Following the Spanish–American War of 1898, in which the United States easily defeated the forces of the old **colonial** power of Spain, the nation even acquired its first colonies, most notably the Philippine Islands in the Pacific. By 1900, the United States had become a global power.

A painting showing Americans celebrating the official dedication of the Statue of Liberty in New York on October 28, 1886. The figure served as a beacon for generations of immigrants coming to the United States from Europe.

Italy opts out

The United States was not the only power to watch the events of August 1914 from the sidelines. Italy had been linked by treaty to the Central Powers since 1882. The **Triple Alliance** was, however, only defensive—Italy only had to support Germany if it was attacked and not if Germany itself was the attacker, a fact that the Italians would call on to avoid declaring war on the Allies in 1914. In fact, Italy joined with the Allies in May 1915.

Because of its global connections, when war finally broke out it was impossible for the United States not to be affected. From the start, U.S. citizens found themselves taking sides. There were eleven million Americans of German or Austro-Hungarian descent, and many of them passionately supported the **Central Powers.** Even so, public opinion generally backed the **Allies,** not at least because so many other Americans traced their origins back to British ancestors. Economic ties with Britain and France also became important as the war dragged on. U.S. trade with these two countries increased dramatically between 1914 and 1916 as the demand for weapons soared.

The giant Carnegie steel works in Pennsylvania in 1905. The United States was the world's fastest-growing economic power in the years leading up to World War I.

Yet those considerations still lay ahead in 1914. At that time, the United States was not in the mood for war. In fact, a popular song of the day was "I Didn't Raise My Boy To Be a Soldier." Also, no military preparations for war had been made. Although the navy was strong, the U.S. army had only about 100,000 regular troops, a tiny force compared with the millions of men who had been called up in Europe.

American neutrality

On August 18, 1914, U.S. President Woodrow Wilson spelled out to the American people his government's position on the war in Europe. He insisted that Americans should be "**neutral** in fact as well as in name, impartial in thought as well as in action . . ."

Shifting Alliances

The **assassination** of Archduke Franz Ferdinand was the trigger for war in 1914, but one reason a local conflict became a world war was the system of **alliances** linking or dividing the great powers. Treaty obligations required Germany to side with Austria-Hungary against Russia over the matter of war with Serbia. But, as we shall see, that wasn't the only reason Germany supported Austria-Hungary. Similarly, it wasn't just **diplomatic** links that led France to take Russia's side.

For centuries, European powers had relied on diplomacy to keep a **balance of power** that would ensure that no one nation could dominate all the others. The treaties that linked different countries together often included secret clauses that stated what particular action each partner in the treaty would take in different crisis situations. These secrets helped to create an atmosphere of international mistrust in which spying was common. In many instances, disloyal officials sold state secrets to other countries.

The way European diplomacy worked can be grouped into three broad phases. The first was the pattern set by Bismarck from 1871 to 1890. The second was the new course set by Kaiser Wilhelm II from 1890 on. The third was the change in British diplomatic policy that took place at the start of the twentieth century.

Bismarck's diplomacy

With the goal of keeping France isolated, Bismarck built up relations with Austria-Hungary. A formal alliance between Germany and Austria-Hungary was struck in 1879, and it was joined three years later by Italy, creating the **Triple Alliance.** Bismarck also realized that it was important to maintain good relations with Russia. In 1873, Germany, Austria-Hungary, and Russia were informally linked in the League of the Three Emperors, which was an arrangement that survived until 1887. The league was then replaced by the secret **Reinsurance Treaty** between Germany and Russia, which guaranteed that the two countries wouldn't go to war with one another.

Even though he left office in 1890, Germany's Otto von Bismarck, seen below in a 1915 painting by Paul Reith, did much to set up the system of alliances that prevailed in Europe up to World War I.

Kaiser Wilhelm's new course

German **foreign policy** changed when Kaiser Wilhelm II came to power in 1888. Eager to make his mark, the new ruler decided to adopt what became known as a "new course" in foreign policy. Unhappy at this change in foreign policy, Bismarck resigned in 1890. Soon after, Wilhelm refused to renew the Reinsurance Treaty, despite persistent Russian attempts to keep it in force. The result was a diplomatic revolution. Within months Russia and France had entered negotiations with each another. By 1893 they formally became **allies.** To Bismarck's alarm, France was no longer isolated. And with hostile powers to east and west, Germany found itself faced with the prospect of someday having to fight a war on two fronts, against France in the west and Russia in the east.

Great Britain's diplomatic revolution

Great Britain began to look vulnerable once the Triple Alliance linking Germany, Austria-Hungary, and Italy was in place. Furthermore, Germany had gained new **colonies** in China, West Samoa, and parts of Africa. That, along with Germany's economic successes, soon made Britain feel pressure to abandon its isolationist position. So from 1900 on, Britain began to look for allies, becoming increasingly linked with other world powers in the process. The first alliance was with Japan in 1902. Then, in 1904, came the **Entente Cordiale,** or "cordial understanding," with France, which settled colonial disputes and marked a new warmth in relations between the two countries. In 1907 a similar agreement was reached with Russia. With Germany and Austria-Hungary on one side, and France, Russia, and Britain on the other, the pattern of the August 1914 crisis had fallen into place.

Britain's King Edward VII salutes the French flag during the 1903 visit that paved the way for the Entente Cordiale, linking the two countries in friendship.

The Schlieffen Plan

The **alliance** system meant that a dispute between any two European powers ran the risk of developing into a confrontation all across Europe. Germany made conflict even more likely in 1905 when it secretly adopted a new military strategy known as the Schlieffen plan. After the Franco-Russian alliance, Germany created the plan because it realized that it might have to fight a war on two fronts.

Waging war on two fronts

The plan was named after Count Alfred von Schlieffen, chief of the German general staff and the highest-ranking military commander from 1891 to 1905. As early as 1892, he realized that Germany might have to divide its military forces in the event of a war. One army would be needed to fight the Russians on the nation's eastern border, and another would have to fight the French in the west. The obvious danger was that Germany's forces, weakened by the split, would be crushed like a nut in a nutcracker.

Russian troops on parade in 1914. German fears of Russian military strength lay behind the formulation of the Schlieffen plan. The plan was designed to avoid the risk of Germany fighting a war on two fronts.

Von Schlieffen's solution was based on the idea that attack is often the best form of defense. He knew that Russia, because of its size and its inefficient transportation system, would be slow to **mobilize** in the event of war. The best estimates suggested that the process would take at least six weeks. The Schlieffen plan proposed that German forces should take advantage of this delay to deliver a knockout blow to France, the enemy in the west. Then, with France defeated, Germany would be free to concentrate all its armies against Russia on the Eastern Front, where they could use their combined might to bring the Russian steamroller to a halt.

However, France had used the years since the Franco-Prussian War to build strong defenses along its border with Germany. A chain of fortresses all the way from Luxembourg to Switzerland was erected to prevent just such an attack. To overcome this problem, the Schlieffen plan proposed bypassing this frontier altogether. Instead, German forces would invade France through Belgium and attack the country's northern frontier. The plan was very specific as to which targets should be reached and taken for each day that it was in operation. The invading army had to keep to a strict timetable, or schedule, if France was to be defeated within the required six weeks.

An act of aggression

One problem with the plan was that since 1839 Belgium had been a **neutral** country, with its neutrality guaranteed by all the major European powers, including Germany. Because Belgium did not take sides, invading it would therefore be an obvious act of aggression. Yet, the plan's authors were not concerned with this detail. Von Schlieffen and his successors assumed, it seems, that the Belgian people would let the German troops pass through without a fight.

When the plan was finally put into action in 1914, however, the Belgians chose instead to resist. The German invasion, along with the attacks on ordinary Belgian civilians, shocked those who up to that point had not taken sides. Germany's invasion of Belgium finally united the people of Great Britain in favor of going to war. The aggression also did much to turn public opinion in the United States against the **Central Powers** and so helped to ensure that when the U.S. did join the conflict, it was on the **Allied** side.

This map shows the planned areas of attack on the Eastern and Western fronts as described in the Schlieffen plan. By the time the plan was finally put into action in 1914, changes had been made by the German commander-in-chief, Helmut von Moltke.

The gist of the plan

General von Schlieffen explained the logic that lay behind his strategy: "*Germany must strive . . . first to strike down one of the allies while the other is kept occupied; but then, when the one [enemy] is conquered, it must, by exploiting its railways, bring a superiority of numbers to the other theater of war, which will also destroy the other enemy.*"

Flash Points Overseas: The Colonies

When countries linked themselves together through formal and informal **alliances,** they did so because they believed such alliances would prevent war. But the alliance system could not stop the competition and **colonial** rivalry that continued to provoke conflict in overseas colonies. Wilhelm II of Germany was determined to get involved in colonial affairs. This only added to the problem. The **Boer War** was one such colonial conflict. It took place in South Africa from 1899 to 1902 between British settlers and the "Boers," which was what the early Dutch and German settlers were called. Germany's support for Great Britain's Boer opponents played a part in souring relations between the two countries and pushing Britain into an alliance with Russia and France.

Targeting North Africa

As the twentieth century got under way, the focus of colonial expansion turned toward North Africa. This was one of the few parts of the continent that had not already been extensively colonized. The region also had great strategic importance because it was so close to Europe.

*The Italian flag is raised over Tripoli, the capital of Libya, in 1911. Italy's success in taking Libya from the Ottomans encouraged the **Balkan** countries to declare war on Turkey the following year.*

The main colonial power in the area in 1900 was France, which had ruled Algeria since 1830 and had strong influence in neighboring Tunisia. The British had a presence in North Africa, having established a **protectorate** over Egypt in 1882. Italy also had ambitions in the region. Seeking to build up an empire of its own, Italy set its sights on Libya, which it finally snatched from **Ottoman** control in 1911.

Crisis in Morocco

One of the few countries in North Africa to successfully maintain its independence was Morocco. Throughout the 19th century, it had been ruled by native **sultans.** But the country became vulnerable after 1894, when the crown passed into the hands of a thirteen-year-old boy.

In 1905, Wilhelm II chose to make a highly publicized visit to Tangier during which he offered the sultan German support for Moroccan independence. This offer was seen as a direct challenge to France. From their base in neighboring Algeria, the French had taken it for granted that Tangier should naturally fall under the French **sphere of influence.** To resolve this **diplomatic** crisis, the Algeciras Conference was convened in 1906. Britain, seeing Germany as its main rival, decided to stand by the **Entente Cordial** and support France. Germany was forced to accept the agreements made at the conference.

A more serious crisis occurred in 1911 when French troops broke the Algeciras agreement. Germany, feeling it had not done enough in the 1905–1906 crisis, took a more aggressive approach this time by sending a gunboat, the *Panther*, to the Moroccan port of Agadir. The act was seen as a direct challenge to France, and for a time there seemed to be a high possibility of war breaking out. Britain declared that it would support France against Germany and put the British naval fleet on alert. Once again, the Germans had to back down. In the negotiations that followed, France agreed to buy off German claims to Morocco by handing over some colonial territories farther south in Africa, in the Congo basin.

The two Moroccan crises were both settled peacefully. It looked as if the alliance system was working. But Britain and Russia had supported France on both occasions. It was beginning to look to the Germans as if their country was in danger of becoming surrounded by hostile powers.

Kaiser Wilhelm II's official visit to Morocco in 1905 set off an international crisis, as France and its ally Britain regarded the country as falling within the French sphere of influence.

The Arms Race

The introduction of the HMS Dreadnought *in 1906 launched a new era in naval shipbuilding. The ship's high speed and the range of its huge guns made all other battleships obsolete.*

In the decade leading up to the war, there was increasing competition between the European powers to match or outdo one another in military might. This increased spending on weapons, in fact, turned out to be self-defeating. As one country built up its army, another would feel the need to do the same. With larger armies and more weapons, the prospect of war in Europe became more likely.

Building more battleships

When Germany decided to build up its own navy at the turn of the century, it was Great Britain who felt most threatened. As the largest **colonial** power, Britain felt it had to maintain its mastery of the seas. At first Britain felt that its naval superiority was so great that there was little chance of the Germans catching up. The British, however, increased the pace of the naval race in

1906 when they introduced a new kind of battleship called the *dreadnought.* The dreadnought's size and speed and its battery of big guns, which could fire farther than those of any previous warship, made all existing battleships obsolete, or no longer of any use.

Suddenly, Germany and Britain found themselves in serious competition when Germany announced that it would build four of the new dreadnoughts. By 1910, however, Britain had, at great expense, established a clear lead in this class of ship, building eleven dreadnoughts to Germany's eight. In 1912 Germany turned its attention to expanding its army.

Call to arms

Germany began building up its army because it realized that the forces of the **Central Powers** were heavily outnumbered by those of Russia and France. Together, the standing armies of Germany and Austria-Hungary numbered about one million men, while those of their two potential enemies reached nearly twice that figure. One reason the size of Germany's army was limited was that for years Germany's **aristocratic** officer group had resisted any sizeable increase that would have opened up their ranks to the middle classes, who the officers despised. Now, however, necessity demanded change, and the German parliament passed a measure designed to boost recruitment immediately by some 60 percent. France responded by increasing its period of **conscription,** or required military service, from two to three years. In turn, Russia announced a "Great Program" designed to enlarge its army by 40 percent over the next three years.

Prussian guards on parade before Kaiser Wilhelm II. By 1914, Germany feared that its army was outnumbered by those of its rivals to the east and west.

Even more alarming from the German point of view, the French agreed to loan money to the Russian government. The money would enable the Russians to build an extra 3,125 miles (5,000 kilometers) of strategic railroad by 1918. Germany's entire Schlieffen plan rested on Russia's being slow to call up its troops, and that situation seemed like it was about to change.

By mid-1914, Germany felt seriously threatened. The military balance seemed to be swinging against the Central Powers. From Germany's viewpoint, if war had to come, the sooner the better.

The hammer or the anvil

Germany's chancellor, Prince Bernhard von Bulow, put the case for expanding the armed forces in a speech he gave in 1899: *"The means of fighting the battle for existence in this world without strong armaments on land and water, for a nation soon to count 60 millions, living in the center of Europe and at the same time stretching out its economic feelers in all directions, have not yet been found. In the coming century the German nation will either be the hammer or the anvil."*

The Balkan Cauldron

Many years before the outbreak of war in 1914, Germany's Iron Chancellor Otto von Bismarck had predicted that "some foolish thing in the **Balkans**" would provide the spark to set all Europe on fire. Events would prove him to be right. The area was like a cauldron, or kettle, about to boil over.

The Balkan region of eastern Europe was made up of many different groups of people, including Greeks, Macedonians, Albanians, Serbs, Croatians, Bosnians, Bulgarians, and Romanians. The Balkan region was ruled by the **Ottoman** Turks, whose power was weakening. Austria-Hungary and Russia both wished to take over the Ottoman Empire's European possessions. But the **Slav** people of this region, influenced by the independent Slav kingdom of Serbia, wanted to rule themselves, free of the control of any **imperial** power. Although Russia had traditionally supported the Slavs' cause, agreements with Austria-Hungary in 1897 and 1903 had kept Russia from offering any help to the Slavs in any possible attempts to gain their independence.

Crisis over Bosnia

This situation changed in 1908 when Austria-Hungary's foreign minister, Count Aehrenthal, decided to **annex** the Slav territory of Bosnia and Herzegovina into the Austro-Hungarian Empire. Russia secretly agreed to the move because Austria-Hungary promised to support Russia on naval issues. Russia had hoped to gain access to the Dardanelles Straits so that the country's warships could reach the Mediterranean Sea. However, Russia never got its side of the deal. Russia's **ally** Serbia was also outraged, because leaders there had hoped to take over these territories for Serbia. As a result, Russia emerged from the situation with its reputation as a champion of the Slav cause badly damaged.

In 1912, full-scale war broke out in the Balkan region. The trigger was Italy's seizure of Libya from Turkey in the previous year, which had shown just how weak the Ottoman regime had become. Serbia, allied with Greece and Bulgaria, then seized control of Ottoman Turkey's Macedonian lands. The allies rapidly achieved total victory, winning almost all of the Ottoman's remaining territories in Europe. They then disagreed over the division of the these territories, and a second Balkan War was fought in 1913, this time with Bulgaria on one side and its two former allies on the other. Bulgaria lost and was forced to hand over many of the gains it had made the previous year.

Serbia victorious

The chief winner from the two wars turned out to be Serbia, which nearly doubled in size. Austria-Hungary watched the Serbs' success with mounting alarm. In the peace conference held in London in May 1913 that brought the first Balkan war to an end, Austria-Hungary used its influence to ensure that Serbia did not get access to the sea, as Serbia desired. It persuaded conference delegates to create the independent kingdom of Albania instead, stretching along the Adriatic coastline. Once more Russia took no action to defend Serbian interests in the face of Austro-Hungarian pressure.

The Balkan Wars set the scene for the archduke's assassination at Sarajevo. In the wake of the Serb advance in 1912, Austria-Hungary had initially wanted to send its army to intervene and had only been persuaded to hold back when its ally Germany refused to lend its support. In 1914 Austria-Hungary still wanted a fight with Serbia. Russia, however, was still hurting from what it regarded as two successive **diplomatic** defeats. Furthermore, neither country was in a mood to compromise, as the events following the **assassination** of Franz Ferdinand would show.

Macedonian civilians drive out occupying Bulgarian troops following the second Balkan War as shown in this newspaper illustration from 1913. In this conflict, Bulgaria lost most of the gains it had made in the previous year.

The Road to War

A magazine illustration reconstructs the moment when a Serbian nationalist shot Archduke Franz Ferdinand and his wife in Sarajevo on June 28, 1914. This assassination set in motion the events that led to the outbreak of war.

On the morning of June 28, 1914, Franz Ferdinand and his wife arrived in the city of Sarajevo in Bosnia and Herzegovina. A first attempt to **assassinate** the archduke was made when a bomb was thrown into his car as it drove toward the town hall. Quick thinking by the archduke, who managed to throw the bomb away, saved their lives, but only for a short time. When the driver of their car took a wrong turn, he accidentally drove into the path of another assassin, who seized the unexpected opportunity and shot both the archduke and his wife dead.

Death in Sarajevo

One of the individuals in the plot to assassinate Archduke Franz Ferdinand described the murder: *"As the car came abreast he [assassin Gavrilo Princip] stepped forward from the curb, drew his automatic pistol from his coat and fired two shots. The first struck the wife of the archduke, the Archduchess Sofia, in the abdomen. She was an expectant mother. She died instantly. The second bullet struck the archduke close to the heart. He uttered only one word, 'Sofia!'—a call to his stricken wife. Then his head fell back and he collapsed."*

It is clear now that the events in Sarajevo triggered the outbreak of the war, but at the time few people guessed that anything so terrible was about to happen. Political assassinations were common at the time. Russia alone had lost a **czar,** a prime minister, and dozens of other officials to the bomb or the bullet over the previous 35 years. After the killing of Franz Ferdinand, most people were shocked but expected Austria-Hungary to come to terms with the loss. Few European political leaders bothered to cancel their summer vacations in expectation of serious trouble.

This time, however, Austria-Hungary was determined to make an example of the Serbs. Knowing that several would-be assassins had been in Sarajevo on the fateful day, the Austro-Hungarian government immediately decided that the assassination had been organized in Serbia. Now the authorities decided that the murders provided an ideal opportunity for crushing Serbia once and for all.

The kaiser's blank check

Before taking action, Austria-Hungary needed to get the support of its powerful German **ally.** On July 5, 1914, Kaiser Wilhelm responded positively with a "blank check" of support. This blank check, so called because it allowed Austria-Hungary to do whatever it wanted, marked the next step on the road to war.

The reasons for Germany's decision in 1914 went well beyond the natural sympathy felt by the kaiser over the death of a fellow royal. It was also shaped by the belief that Austria-Hungary must be seen to take firm action if the nation was to keep its standing among the great powers. Germany also expected that because Russia was fiercely antiterrorist, it would sympathize more with Austria-Hungary than with Serbia. Not expecting war, the kaiser happily set off next day on a three-week cruise in the Baltic Sea.

A nation ready for war

There were other considerations behind the German decision to support Austria-Hungary. Germany had just completed an eight-year project to widen its Kiel Canal, which links the Baltic and the North Seas, so that **dreadnought**-sized battleships could pass through the canal without going around Denmark. Germany's military planners knew that, if war should come, their position against France and Great Britain was as good as it was ever likely to be. Germany's commander-in-chief, Helmut von Moltke, had recently told his Austrian counterpart, "We are ready, and the sooner the better for us." Germany's leaders may not have expected a European war when they issued the blank check, but they were well prepared for war should it come.

Kaiser Wilhelm (center) attends military maneuvers with his commander-in-chief, Helmut von Moltke, early in 1914. When the time came, it was von Moltke who was responsible for putting the Schlieffen plan into action.

Ultimatum to Serbia

For 25 days it appeared to the public that little was being done about the murders in Sarajevo. Behind the scenes in Vienna, the capital of Austria, though, frenzied **diplomatic** activity was under way. One reason for the delay was that at first the government could not agree about which course to take. Also, the government wanted the nation's farmers to have time to bring in the harvest before possibly being called up to serve in a war.

Finally, on July 23, 1914, Austria-Hungary delivered its **ultimatum,** or list of demands, to Serbia. The ultimatum was expressed in such strong language that it made war almost inevitable. The Serbs were asked to crack down on all organizations considered hostile to Austria-Hungary and to arrest those involved with them. They were also asked to allow Austro-Hungarian police and military into Serbia to help hunt them down. Serbia was given just two days to accept the terms or face war. Eager to avoid that risk, the Serbs indicated that they were prepared to consider all the demands except the presence of Austro-Hungarian police in their territory. Seizing upon that refusal to allow the police in Serbia, the authorities in Vienna at once rejected the reply.

Austria-Hungary declares war

Suddenly, all of Europe realized the seriousness of the crisis. Still, on July 26, a general war still seemed like it was a long way off. Similar confrontations in the past had been settled by diplomacy, and now Sir Edward Grey, the British foreign minister, proposed a conference of all the powers at which the issues could be worked out. This time, however, Austria-Hungary was in no mood to settle the crisis through debate with other countries, and Germany backed Austria-Hungary's stand. On July 28, Austria-Hungary formally declared war on Serbia. The Serb capital of Belgrade was bombed the following day.

German soldiers listen to a lecture on airplane engines in early 1914. World War I was the first conflict in which aviation played a significant part.

Gauging the Russian reaction

All eyes now turned to St. Petersburg to see Russia's reaction. Would the **czar's** government stand by while its Serb **ally** was attacked, or would it send troops to intervene? There were strong arguments against getting involved. The "Great Program" to expand the army had barely gotten under way. Also, previous wars had not gone well for Russia and had led to popular outcries against the czar's rule. Encouraged by assurances of French support, the czar did not hesitate for long. On July 29, he gave orders for Russian forces to **mobilize** against Austria-Hungary. A confrontation between two of the great powers now seemed inevitable, but hope remained that it could still be limited to Austria-Hungary and Russia. Frantic diplomatic efforts continued to prevent the other powers from becoming involved.

On August 2, 1914, crowds gather in Berlin to listen to an army officer announcing that Germany had declared war on Russia.

COUNTDOWN TO WAR

THE KEY DATES OF THE 1914 CRISIS WERE:

JUNE 28 — ASSASSINATION OF FRANZ FERDINAND IN SARAJEVO
JULY 5 — KAISER WILHELM GIVES THE "BLANK CHECK" TO AUSTRIA-HUNGARY
JULY 23 — AUSTRIA-HUNGARY DELIVERS ULTIMATUM TO SERBIA
JULY 28 — AUSTRIA-HUNGARY DECLARES WAR ON SERBIA
JULY 30 — RUSSIA ORDERS GENERAL MOBILIZATION
AUGUST 1 — GERMANY DECLARES WAR ON RUSSIA
AUGUST 3 — GERMANY DECLARES WAR ON FRANCE
AUGUST 3 — GERMAN TROOPS INVADE BELGIUM
AUGUST 4 — BRITAIN DECLARES WAR ON GERMANY

Timetables to War

In the end, some of the key decisions that turned a local war in Serbia into a European war centered on a most unlikely factor: railroads. Railroads were connected with military planning in Russia, Germany, and France. In each of these countries, generals were convinced that speed was of vital importance in responding to any military threat. At a time when motor transportation was still a novelty, armies were moved rapidly by train. Stressing the need for mobility, a German military saying of the late nineteenth century was, "Build no more fortresses; build railways." When **Czar** Nicholas II gave the order for Russian armies to be called up, near panic spread through Europe's foreign ministries. In Germany, Wilhelm II was particularly alarmed, because he had expected Russia to stand down.

All or nothing for Russia

Kaiser Wilhelm of Germany asked Czar Nicholas II, his distant cousin, to stop Russian **mobilization.** In exchange, the kaiser promised he would put pressure on Austria-Hungary to negotiate over Serbia. For a moment it seemed that his **diplomacy** might work, because Nicholas gave orders that Russian troops should be called up only on the Austro-Hungarian border, not the German one. Within hours, though, the order was changed. Nicholas had learned from his generals that Russia's military planning simply did not allow for a limited mobilization. It had to be all or nothing or the call-up would fail.

In Germany, railroad schedules, or timetables, were also an important military concern. The entire Schlieffen plan depended on getting the right troops to the right place at the right time. General mobilization involved no fewer than 11,000 trains, all of them traveling to an exact schedule. So when Wilhelm tried to limit the conflict by asking for troops to be called only to the Russian front to avert the risk of war with France, he too was informed that it could not be done. A general war, it seemed, could not be avoided because years of military planning had made it inevitable.

Crowds gather in the rain to watch German troops as they march into the Belgian capital city of Brussels in August 1914. Resistance to the German invasion led to many Belgian civilians being killed.

Would Britain fight?

The final uncertainties concerned Great Britain and Italy. Italy had been part of the **Triple Alliance** with Germany and Austria-Hungary since 1879, but only for purposes of defense. Britain was linked to France and Russia by two separate **ententes,** but had no firm treaty obligations forcing it to fight. Although Sir Edward Grey, the British foreign minister, must have thought war was coming, a majority of the British **cabinet** was against getting involved in a continental conflict.

In Great Britain, the government seemed willing to act in favor of war only in the case of obvious, unprovoked aggression. Realizing the importance of the issue, the French government pulled its troops six miles (ten kilometers) back from the German border to prevent any suggestion that France had started the fighting.

The German invasion of the **neutral** country of Belgium on August 3 as part of the Schlieffen plan finally turned the tide of British public opinion. Germany had already declared war on Russia and France, and now Britain declared war on Germany. That same day, Italy announced that it would remain neutral. At this stage, Germany, Russia, France, Austria-Hungary, and Britain were at war. Soldiers from the British and French empires would soon be shipped to Europe to take part in the fighting. In the months and years to come, other nations would be drawn into the conflict.

In World War I, trains were an important way of moving troops to the front line. In this picture, the troops on the train are Serbian. At first the Serbs had some successes against Austro-Hungarian forces, but they were finally crushed by a joint German-Austrian campaign late in 1915.

Why Did the War Last So Long?

Most of the decision-makers in August 1914 expected a short war. British troops went to war expecting to be home by Christmas. The kaiser in Germany went one step further and told troops leaving for the front line in August that they would be back "before the leaves have fallen from the trees."

The collapse of the Schlieffen plan

The war would indeed have been short if the Schlieffen plan had worked, but it did not. Belgian resistance slowed down the initial assault. Then, Russia surprised the military planners by invading eastern Germany earlier than expected. German troops had to be moved east to meet the threat. In a decisive battle, the French held the German forces at the Marne River, northeast of Paris. On September 10, one day short of the six weeks allowed in Germany's plan for the capture of Paris, von Moltke had to order a limited German retreat.

The battlefronts of central Europe during World War One.

The two sides then competed in a desperate race west—the so-called Race to the Sea. By October, both sides on the Western Front were dug in behind continuous lines of fortifications that stretched 500 miles (800 kilometers) from the Swiss border to the English Channel.

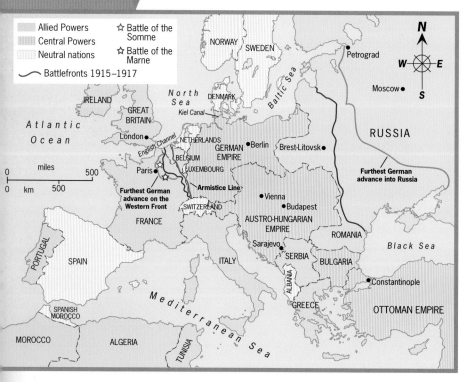

A blood-soaked balance of power

Once the trenches had been dug, the very **balance of power** that had been meant to guarantee peace instead ensured a long war. The rival **alliances** roughly balanced out, preventing either side from winning a decisive advantage. On paper, the **Allies** had greater reserves of manpower. Over the course of the war, they would call on the services of 40 million soldiers, while the **Central Powers** called up 25 million. In the early years, however, the Central Powers had a slight advantage, thanks to Germany's central location, which meant it could move troops efficiently between fronts as they were needed to meet new challenges.

The Germans' early victories in the west also meant that they simply had to hold onto their gains, while the burden of driving them back fell on the Allies. In the conditions of warfare at the time, attack was more costly than defense. Men armed with rifles and bayonets who went "over the top" of the trenches to attack soldiers who had machine guns and were dug into trenches regularly suffered at least a third more **casualties** than the defenders.

War on the Eastern Front

On the Eastern Front, the fighting was less bogged down than in the west. There, the early Russian gains were soon reversed, and German troops advanced far into Russian territory in Poland and even into Russia itself. There were, however, still long periods of **stalemate** on both fronts. With neither side willing to back down, thousands, then millions, of soldiers were killed.

This staged photograph illustrates how to survive poison gas attacks by wearing gas masks. Poison gas was used as a weapon on the Western Front from 1915 on.

New weapons

In 1915 the Germans shocked world opinion by turning to chemical warfare in the form of **poison gas.** The following year saw the first tanks in action—they were used to lead attacks on the trenches. Probably the most important development in warfare was air power. Once bombs could be dropped from the air, civilians as well as soldiers found themselves caught up in the conflict.

The United States Tips the Balance

Throughout 1915 and 1916, the generals tried everything in their power to break the military **stalemate.** Both sides repeatedly sought and failed to smash through enemy lines with all-out assaults. Bloodbaths such as the Battle of the Somme were the result. At sea, the British imposed a naval **blockade** on the **Central Powers** that prevented vital supplies from getting through.

Each side also looked for new **allies.** The war spread beyond Europe when Japan joined the Allied side in August 1914. Two months later, Ottoman Turkey came to the aid of the Central Powers. Lured by the promise of big gains in North Africa and elsewhere, Italy finally entered the war in May 1915, on the Allied side. In the same year, Bulgaria cast in its lot with Germany and Austria-Hungary. By far the most important new entrant, though, was the United States, which in April 1917 entered the war on the Allied side. U.S. President Woodrow Wilson had long resisted getting involved, having won the 1916 presidential election with the promise of keeping the United States out of the war.

Crowds gather in London to welcome the arrival of U.S. troops in 1917. By the middle of 1918, 250,000 American soldiers were crossing the Atlantic each month.

The submarine menace

One reason the United States entered the conflict was Germany's use of submarine warfare. In an attempt to counter the British naval blockade, German military leaders had authorized the use of the newly invented **U-boats** against unarmed Allied **merchant ships.** Any ship suspected of trading with the Allies could be sunk without warning. Some of the civilian **casualties** that resulted were U.S. citizens, notably 128 of the 1,195 passengers and crew on board the British liner *Lusitania,* sunk in the Atlantic in May 1915. German planners realized that the move would almost certainly bring the United States into the war. However, they also believed that if they could starve Great Britain out by preventing food supplies from reaching British ports, this would outweigh the risk of U.S. intervention.

Another incident that pushed the United States to declare war was the Zimmerman telegram. Arthur Zimmerman, Germany's foreign minister, sent a coded message in a telegram to a German diplomat in Mexico. The message suggested that if Mexico joined the Central Powers, it would be given territory in the United States. The British secret service intercepted the message and eagerly passed it on to U.S. authorities. When the message became public, Americans were outraged, and more of them saw the need to enter the war.

The United States' declaration of war had little immediate impact, because there were few U.S. troops ready to enter the combat. In the summer of 1917, a more important development was Britain's use of **convoys** of armed escorts for merchant ships, which counteracted the U-boat threat.

Germany's last push for victory

Even so, late 1917 and early 1918 saw Germany come closer to outright victory than at any time since the start of the conflict. In 1917, the unstable Russian monarchy fell, and within months a **communist** government took over. The nation's new leaders agreed to sign a peace treaty at Brest-Litovsk in Poland that gave Germany large areas of Russian land. Encouraged by this success, the German high command determined to use its last reserves to push for final victory in the west. In the spring and summer of 1918, they almost succeeded, advancing to within 38 miles (60 kilometers) of Paris.

But the Allied line held, and the German army had nothing left to throw at it. At this point U.S. reinforcements proved decisive. There were nearly two million U.S. troops in Europe by the end of the war. The Allies launched a series of counterattacks that forced the Germans back. By the end of August, the German troops had lost all their earlier gains and were still retreating.

A German poster illustrates the effectiveness of U-boats, or submarines, in sinking Allied ships. Attacks on merchant ships helped bring the United States into the war. The German text in the poster reads "Forward the U-boats!"

The Peace That Never Was

The war was by now turning against the **Central Powers** in other areas. Bulgaria surrendered to the **Allies** in September, soon followed by Ottoman Turkey and Austria-Hungary. With the Western Front buckling under Allied pressure, German authorities realized that the game was up. On November 8, Germany requested an **armistice.** On November 9, Kaiser Wilhelm abdicated, or gave up the throne. Two days later, the guns finally fell silent. World War I was over.

Though a wave of relief greeted the end of the fighting, rejoicing was limited, even on the winning side. Too many people had died to make for easy celebrations. The mood was further dampened by an economic downturn caused by the sudden closing of war industries and a worldwide flu epidemic that killed almost as many people as the war itself.

The Fourteen Points

People everywhere spoke of the conflict as the "war to end war," and there was general agreement that the world had changed remarkably. Yet few had any clear idea of what the new world order would look like. One person who did have an idea, though, was U.S. President Woodrow Wilson, who had outlined his proposals for peace to the U.S. Congress in January 1918. The "Fourteen Points" he put forward sketched a future based on **democracy** and the right of small nations to determine their own destiny. Blaming Europe's secret treaties, at least in part, for the outbreak of war, he also insisted on open **diplomacy,** along with **free trade** and steps toward **disarmament.**

The program was somewhat farsighted, but in 1918 it fell largely on deaf ears. To war-weary European statesmen, the "war to end war" meant crushing their enemies so they couldn't threaten European peace again.

Making Germany pay

In 1918, with millions of deaths to justify, victorious France and Great Britain hardly felt generous. Britain's prime minister David Lloyd-George won reelection that year on a policy of "making Germany pay." France's premier Georges Clemenceau was understandably obsessed with the

A painting by Sir William Orpen shows ministers gathered to sign the Treaty of Versailles in June 1919. The setting was the Hall of Mirrors, where the German Empire had been declared in 1871.

danger a revived Germany might pose. He demanded severe restrictions on Germany's military strength as well as a zone along the border with France, the Rhineland, in which all military installations would be banned. When the United States refused to cancel Allied **war debts,** Clemenceau also demanded reparations from Germany to pay for the cost of the war.

The Treaty of Versailles, signed in 1919, in many ways delivered the worst of all worlds. The German public was outraged. People who had been expecting victory just three months earlier and who had thought they were negotiating from a strong position now felt betrayed.

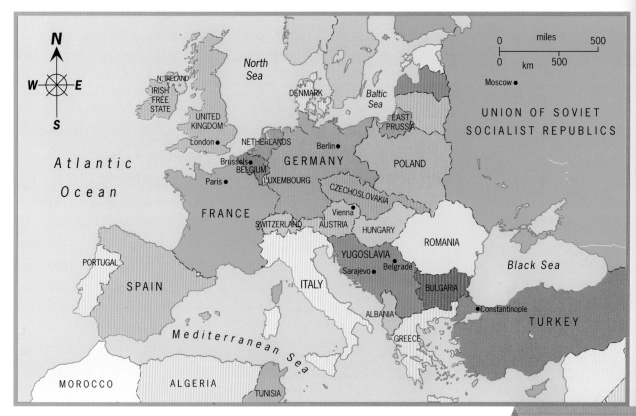

The countries of Europe between World War I and World War II.

Germany was weakened by the settlement, which returned Alsace and Lorraine to France as well as some eastern territories to a newly independent Poland. But Germany was not fatally wounded. With the breakup of the Austro-Hungarian and **Ottoman** Empires to its east and south, which had occurred as a result of the war, its strategic position was in many ways stronger. Alarmingly for France, the prestige of the German military was also still as high as ever.

Not only did Germany now have grounds for seeking revenge but it was also in a stronger position to do so. Far from putting an end to war, the Versailles settlement had actually paved the way for the rise of Adolf Hitler and **Nazism** and for the outbreak of a second world war just twenty years later.

Learning the Lessons

The world that emerged from World War I was very different from the world of 1914. The great empires of Europe had disappeared forever with the overthrow of the **czar** in Russia and the collapse of Austria-Hungary. Germany also had lost its kaiser and had been reborn, for a time, as a **democratic republic.**

A discharged soldier begs for money on the street in London in the 1920s. Across Europe, the war left many social problems in its wake.

The victorious powers were different, too, even if the changes were not quite so obvious. To start with, most of the **allies** were poorer. The war had been very costly, and to pay the bills, both France and Great Britain had borrowed heavily. There had been social changes, as well. Women had taken over men's jobs when the men had been called up to fight, and their economic status had risen accordingly. Women's efforts during the war also contributed to their gaining the right to vote in some countries. In addition, **labor unions** had increased their influence, having been treated as partners by governments to boost the war effort.

Building a new world order

Some first steps were taken in the direction of Woodrow Wilson's new world order. The League of Nations, which was the forerunner of today's United Nations, was set up to provide an organization in which countries could settle disputes by discussion rather than by fighting. But the League's effectiveness was always limited, above all because the U.S. Congress, weary of foreign entanglements, refused to let the United States join. Without U.S. backing, the League looked too much like a European club—and one dominated by the war's victors at that.

Even so, the League marked a move toward a world in which reason rather than brute force would shape international relations. It set up the Permanent Court of International Justice in the Dutch city of The Hague to try cases that crossed national borders. Some people wanted to bring the kaiser and his generals to trial for such lethal innovations as the use of **poison gas** and unrestricted submarine warfare, as well as for the invasion of **neutral** Belgium. However, the days when heads of state could be called to account for their actions were still to come in the future.

Losers and winners

Even leaving aside its terrible human cost, World War I effectively shattered the political ambitions of most of the nations that fought in it. The emperors of Germany and Austria-Hungary had sought to increase their own prestige and the status of their empires, only to come out of the struggle without their

thrones and with their realms in ruins. Great Britain had fought to maintain its position as a **colonial** power, but in 1918 it found itself economically weakened. Its global position was damaged as well as its empire, which would in fact be gone within the next 50 years. France, which had fought for security from its mighty German neighbor, could take some comfort from winning back Alsace and Lorraine. But it emerged from the peace settlement to find Germany angry and still untamed and ready to fight again just two decades later.

Delegates gather for the opening session of the League of Nations in Geneva, Switzerland, in 1920. The League paved the way for today's United Nations.

If World War I had any type of economic winner, it was probably the United States. The United States alone had the kind of war that the other powers had dreamed of back in 1914—short and victorious. The nation had been on the rise industrially before that time, but the extra boost given to its economy by British and French demand for war supplies had brought boom times to its factories. The United States had demonstrated its military prowess, and its industries now led the world. Each of the European powers had gone to war with the expectation of increasing its power and prestige. Instead, Europe succeeded only in paving the way for the United States to rise as the greatest power in the twentieth century.

Timeline

1871	German Empire proclaimed in the Palace of Versailles
	France loses Alsace and Lorraine to Germany after their defeat in the **Franco-Prussian War**
1872	League of the Three Emperors is formed between Germany, Russia, and Austria-Hungary
1879	Germany and Austria-Hungary create the Dual Alliance
1882	**Triple Alliance**—Italy joins the German and Austro-Hungarian alliance
1887	**Reinsurance Treaty** signed between Germany and Russia
1888	Wilhelm II becomes Germany's kaiser, or emperor
1890	Resignation of German chancellor, Otto von Bismarck
	Germany refuses to renew Reinsurance Treaty with Russia
1894	Franco-Russian alliance is signed
1897	Austria-Hungary and Russia agree to keep the peace in the **Balkans**
1898	First German naval law introduced, which launches naval arms race with Great Britain
	Fashoda Incident sets Britain against France
1899	Britain goes to war with South Africa's **Boers** (to 1902)
1900	Second German naval law
1902	British-Japanese alliance formed
1903	New, more **nationalistic dynasty** seizes power in Serbia
1904	Russo-Japanese War (to 1905)
	Entente Cordiale between France and Britain
1905	First Moroccan crisis pits France against Germany (to 1906)
1906	The Algeciras Conference
1907	HMS **Dreadnought** launched
1907	British-Russian agreement signed
1908	Austria-Hungary annexes Bosnia and Herzegovina
1911	Second Moroccan crisis
	Italy goes to war with Turkey over Libya (to 1912)
1912	First Balkan War (to 1913)
1913	Second Balkan War
1914	Assassination of Archduke Franz Ferdinand in Sarajevo
	Outbreak of World War I
1915	Italy joins the war on the **Allied** side
	German **U-boat** blockade of Britain begins; *Lusitania* sunk
1916	Bulgaria joins the **Central Powers;** Romania joins the Allies
	Battle of the Somme

1917	Zimmerman telegram intercepted
	Russian Revolution. **Czar** overthrown in March; **communists** seize power in November
	United States enters war on Allied side
1918	Treaty of Brest-Litovsk signed between Germany and Russia
	U.S. President Woodrow Wilson outlines his Fourteen Points for peace
	Germany signs **armistice,** bringing World War I to an end
1919	Treaty of Versailles
1920	League of Nations meets for the first time

Further Reading

Curie, Stephen. *Life in the Trenches.* San Diego, Calif.: Lucent Books, 2002.

Dowswell, Paul. *Weapons and Technology of World War I.* Chicago: Heinemann Library, 2002.

Gawne, Jonathan. *Over There!: The American Soldier in World War I.* Broomall, Pa.: Chelsea House Publishers, 1999.

Livesay, Anthony, and John MacDonald. *Great Battles of World War I.* New York: Smithmark Publishers, 1997.

Rees, Rosemary. *The Western Front.* Chicago: Heinemann Library, 1998.

Ross, Stewart. *Assassination in Sarajevo: The Trigger for World War I.* Chicago: Heinemann Library, 2001.

Ross, Stewart. *Causes and Consequences of World War I.* Austin, Tex.: Raintree Publishers, 1998.

Taylor, David. *Key Battles of World War I.* Chicago: Heinemann Library, 2001.

Glossary

alliance link between countries who wish to support one another

allies countries that support one another during peacetime and sometimes during war. During World War I, the Allies included Great Britain, France, Russia, the United States, Italy, and others.

annexation taking control of another country or territory

aristocracy people of high social rank whose position in society is usually inherited from their parents

armistice agreement that ends fighting

assassination murder for political reasons

balance of power political doctrine aimed at ensuring that no one nation is strong enough to dominate its neighbors

Balkans mountain range that a large region of southeastern Europe is named after

blockade use of warships to stop vessels entering an enemy's ports

Boer War South Africans mostly of Dutch or German descent (Boers), who fought a war against the British (1899–1902)

cabinet group of chief ministers chosen to decide government policy

casualty person who is killed or wounded

Central Powers Germany and Austria-Hungary

colonial describing the policy of the more powerful countries to take control of weaker or less developed parts of the world

communist someone who believes in communism, a political system in which the state controls property, industry, and trade

conscription required service in the armed forces

convoy a group of ships sailing together and protected by a warship called a "destroyer"

Crimean War war fought from 1853 to 1856 between Russia on one side and Britain, France, and Turkey on the other

czar emperor of Russia

democracy political system in which the government of a country is elected by its people

diplomacy discussions with other countries that are intended to promote friendly relations

disarmament agreed reduction in stockpiles of weapons

dreadnought heavily armed battleship introduced in 1906

dynasty succession of rulers coming from the same family

Entente Cordiale informal alliance linking Britain and France after 1904

foreign policy government policy concerning its relations with other countries

Franco-Prussian War war in which France fought against Germany in 1870–71

free trade to be able to trade with any country without paying extra charges

hierarchy ranking people one above another according to the power of their position

illiterate being unable to read or write

imperial to do with an empire and its rulers

Industrial Revolution movement in the eighteenth and nineteenth centuries that turned Britain and other powers into industrial nations

industrialization policy of encouraging the development of heavy industry

labor union organization set up to promote the rights of working people

merchant shipping ships carrying trade goods

mobilization calling up of soldiers for war

nationalism belief that people's first loyalty is to their own national group

nation-state country in which all the inhabitants speak the same language and share the same customs and past history

Nazism extreme political views of the National Socialist Party in Germany during Hitler's time

neutral not involved in a conflict

no-man's-land wasteland between opposing lines of trenches in World War I

Ottoman dynasty of sultans ruling Turkey and its empire from 1280 to 1924

patriotism love and loyalty for one's country

poison gas lethal gas used as a weapon

principality small state ruled by a prince rather than a king

protectorate country under the official protection of another country

raked refers to the sweeping movement used by soldiers using machine guns

raw materials naturally occurring materials such as iron ore that can be used by industry to manufacture products

Reinsurance Treaty secret treaty signed in 1887 in which Germany and Russia promised not to go to war against each other

reparations payments from a losing power to a victor to cover the costs of a war

republicanism belief in having an elected president as head of a country rather than an unelected monarch or ruler

Slav East European who speaks Slavonic languages. Russians, Serbs, and Bosnians are Slavs.

sphere of influence countries or territories that other countries feel they have a right to interfere with or rule

stalemate term (originally from chess) for a situation in which neither side can win

sultan Muslim ruler

theater of war area of land in which fighting is taking place

Third Republic system of government in France from 1870 to 1940

Triple Alliance alliance secretly agreed upon between Germany, Austria-Hungary, and Italy in 1882

U-boat German submarine

ultimatum final warning threatening war

war debt debts run up in the course of fighting a war

Index